KILLER INSECTS

KILLER INSECTS

by Don Causey

FRANKLIN WATTS
NEW YORK | LONDON | TORONTO | 1979

TO FRANCINE

Photographs courtesy of: Animals, Animals (Wil-
liard Luce): p. 3, (Leonard La Rue III): p. 35,
(Carson Baldwin Jr.): p. 38; New York Public
Library Picture Collection: pp. 10, 14, 26, 28, 44,
45, 56, 63, 75, 78; The Walters Art Gallery: p. 8;
United Press International: p. 19; Annan Photo
Features: pp. 24, 31, 67; Photo Trends (Oxford
Scientific Films): p. 53; Armed Forces Institute
of Pathology: pp. 59, 68; Panama Canal Company:
p. 64; Center for Disease Control: p. 76.

Library of Congress Cataloging in Publication Data

Causey, Don.
Killer insects.

Bibliography: p.
Includes index.
SUMMARY: Discusses insects that can be called
killers, including rat fleas, bees, wasps, hornets,
yellow jackets, killer bees, tsetse flies, mosquitoes,
army ants, and the kissing bug.
1.   Insects, Injurious and beneficial—Juvenile
literature. 2.   Insects as carriers of diseases—
Juvenile literature. 3.   Dangerous animals—Juvenile literature. [1. Insects, Injurious and beneficial. 2. Dangerous animals] I. Title.
QL468.8.C38   595.7′06′5   79–14482
ISBN 0–531–02924–7

Contents

KILLER INSECTS

Chapter 1
Common and
Uncommon
Insects

Insects are one of the most common forms of life on earth. Just think of the different kinds you have seen right around your home. Certainly you've seen ants and wasps, and, if you have a lawn or garden, you've probably seen grasshoppers and maybe even beetles with bright red spots on their backs.

With insects so common, most people haven't thought much about the fact that some insects are very dangerous. Throughout history, and up until this very minute, certain insects have been killing people and spreading disease. One of the many types of mosquitoes, for example, is currently blamed for one million deaths each year in various parts of the world, and for ten times that many cases of various illnesses.

Another insect, a simple flea very much like the kind that is attracted to dogs, has killed many millions of people by spreading a disease called bubonic plague. Years ago, during an outbreak of the plague in Europe, it is believed that more than 25 million people died. Today in some parts of the world, people are still dying from this flea-borne disease.

All of this is not to suggest that insects kill only by spreading disease. Take the so-called killer bee, for example, which was mistakenly allowed to go free in Brazil after being brought to that country from Africa. Though many of the stories about these insects have been exaggerated, killer bees have occasionally killed children and adults by attacking in sudden, angry swarms. In one episode in São Paulo, Brazil, a swarm of killer bees descended on a schoolyard where a group of children were playing. The children, crying from their stings, ran into the school while officials called the police. To get the insects to leave, the Brazilian government had to call in soldiers with flamethrowers.

Insects such as the killer bee, the flea that causes bubonic plague, and the mosquito are the subject of this book. Before looking at each one in more detail, it should be pointed out that most insects are not only helpful, but are necessary to life on earth. Honeybees, for example, help people live by pollinating (fertilizing) plants. Without their effort, many of the plant foods we eat would not be available. And, certainly, without honeybees, there would be no honey to eat.

Other insects serve as food for birds and fish and therefore indirectly provide humans with food. Still other insects improve the quality of the soil, enabling crops to grow better.

Some insects are actually eaten by people. In some parts of the world, grasshoppers and ants are eaten either fried or covered with chocolate.

A HONEYBEE ATOP THE
FLOWER OF A DUTCH IRIS.

There are also insects that are simply beautiful to look at. The butterfly, for example, is a harmless and pleasant insect to have around. So is the graceful, long-necked praying mantis, which looks—with its tiny "hands" clasped and its head bowed—a little like a person saying a prayer.

So, it is not necessary to worry about all the insects in the world. There are, in fact, only a few out of the thousands and thousands of kinds of insects that can be called killers. But it's interesting and important to know which ones they are.

WHAT IS AN INSECT?

When scientists refer to "an insect," they are talking about a specific group of small animals that, when full-grown, have the following characteristics:

- They breathe air.
- They have three pairs of legs and, usually, two pairs of wings.
- They have bodies separated into three distinct parts called the head, the thorax, and the abdomen.

It's important to know these characteristics of an insect because it explains why some very well-known insectlike killers are not included in this book. Black widow spiders, for example, are not included even though they can certainly kill a person. The brown recluse spider, another killer, is also left out, as is the scorpion, and the tick that causes Rocky Mountain spotted fever. All of these creatures are small animals called arachnids. Though closely related to insects, arachnids are nonetheless different enough to be put in a separate class.

Insects are the most numerous and various forms of life on earth. Scientists have already discovered about 700,000 different kinds of insects, and there is speculation that close to ten million may one day be described.

So how many individual insects are there in the whole world? Obviously, the total number of insects is staggering. It's anybody's guess how big a stack all the insects in the world would make, but it's a safe bet that the stack would be as tall as a mountain and probably heavier than all the people in the world put together.

It is the abundance of insects, as much as anything else, that makes them a little frightening to everyone at times. Fiction writers and movie directors have capitalized on this fear by creating stories about huge cockroaches and massive swarms of man-eating bees. Other writers have imagined big, carnivorous ants the size of cows that swarm over the earth eating people.

Such stories are completely false, of course. Mentioning them, however, does bring us back to the subject of this book: the small number of insects that kill or harm people.

Let's look at the oriental rat flea first.

Chapter 2
Plague!

Imagine for a moment that a flea has just hopped onto the page of this book and has begun to crawl toward your hand. Chances are you wouldn't even realize it, because a typical flea is not too much bigger than the period at the end of this sentence. It's hard to believe that an insect this tiny is the culprit in one of the great horror stories of all times, the outbreak of bubonic plague.

Bubonic plague, also called the black death, is a fatal and highly contagious disease that began to break out for the first recorded time nearly 1,500 years ago. Since then, the black death has killed many millions of people all over the world.

In the fourteenth century, the black death killed between two-thirds and three-fourths of the population in many areas of Europe. And, in 1665, during what came to be called the Great Plague of London, an estimated 68,596 people died in that city alone from bubonic plague.

During the great epidemic of 1894, the black death moved swiftly across China and India, and from there on to the Middle East, Europe, and the United States. By 1917, when the disease tapered off, it had literally spread around the entire world and had killed more than nine million people.

A GRIM STORY

One of the best descriptions of the black death and the effect it had on people was written by Giovanni Boccaccio, an Italian writer who, in 1348, saw the plague kill an estimated 100,000 people in the city of Florence:

> . . . its earliest symptoms in men and women alike was the appearance of certain swellings in the groin or the armpit, some of which were egg-shaped whilst others were roughly the size of the common apple. . . . From the two areas already mentioned, this swelling would begin to spread and within a short time it would appear at random all over the body. Later on, the symptoms of the disease changed and many people began to find dark blotches and bruises on their arms, thighs, and other parts of the body. . . . In most cases death occurred within three days from the appearance of the symptoms we have described, some people dying more rapidly than others. . . .

Bubonic plague also usually causes a high fever, shivering, vomiting, and terrible pain that has been described as "tearing or sharply cutting." The tongue of plague victims often turns yellowish or brown and becomes very dry. It's not unusual for plague victims to become delirious as well, and imagine strange things happening before their eyes.

The main horror of bubonic plague, though, is the large number of people it kills in a short time. Some of the grimmest stories in the world have been told by survivors of plague epidemics. Boccaccio, for example, tells us that so many people died in Florence that there were not enough graves, or enough people to take bodies to the cemetery. Consequently, bodies often stayed in the street for days on end. Those that were taken to gravesites were mostly thrown in ditches together in piles of 100 or more.

Here is one final quote from Boccaccio to suggest what the horror was like in Florence:

> Many dropped dead in the open streets, both by day and by night, whilst a great many others, though lying in their house, drew . . . attention to the fact more by the smell of their rotting corpses than by any other means. And what with these and the others who were dying all over the city, bodies were here there and everywhere.

All of this misery, as mentioned earlier, is the fault of the flea. More specifically, it is the fault of a single type of flea called the oriental rat flea or, scientifically, *Xenopsylla cheopis*. This flea (and sometimes others) spreads bubonic plague by biting people and infecting them with bacillus called *Pasturella pestis*.

THIS PAINTING, ENTITLED
*ST. SEBASTIAN INTERCEDING
FOR THE PLAGUE-STRICKEN,*
SHOWS THE HORROR AND GRIEF
THAT ACCOMPANIED THE PLAGUE
AS IT SWEPT THROUGH EUROPE
IN THE FOURTEENTH CENTURY.

Actually the blame for bubonic plague must be shared by another animal, the ordinary rat. The fact that fleas and rats must team up to cause an outbreak of the plague is something that scientists have known about for only some seventy years. It's easy to imagine, though, how terrified people must have been during plague epidemics before it was known what was causing people to die and what could be done to stop the misery and death.

Boccaccio left an account of people blaming God or the stars for the sickness. Some people, he wrote, believed the disease was caused by something in the air and went about the city holding flowers or spices to their noses.

It was 1894, to be exact, when the black death bacillus was finally identified, and it was a decade after that when the role of rat fleas and rats was fully understood. The full story of the spread of this disease by rats and rat fleas is fascinating.

A DRAWING OF A COSTUME
WORN BY DOCTORS IN THE
SOUTH OF FRANCE DURING
THE PLAGUE OF 1720.

Chapter 3
The Role of
the Rat Flea
and the Rat

The best way to understand how bubonic plague spreads to human beings is to think of ordinary domestic rats as the *reservoir* of this disease and to think of fleas as the *pipeline* that carries it to humans. Fleas serve as a pipeline by biting a rat infected with plague bacillus and later biting a human being.

Go back for a moment to the beginning of Chapter 2 and pick up with the thought that a rat flea has hopped onto the page of this book. With the naked eye all you would see, as mentioned earlier, is a small speck. Up close, though, with a magnifying glass, this speck would take on some unusual features that explain why fleas work so well as a pipeline for bubonic plague.

The most important feature that would spring into view under a magnifying glass would be the mouthparts of the flea. They are specially designed to drill through the skin of an animal and, like a miniature oil well, suck away at the blood inside. Next in importance would be the back legs of the flea. Long, hairy, and amazingly strong, these back legs allow a flea to jump a long distance.

The oriental rat flea, then, is a perfect pipeline for bubonic plague. Driven by a never-ending hunger for blood, it drills through the skin of an infected rat and takes in a small amount of blood, along with a deadly portion of plague bacillus. When the rat dies from the disease, the flea merely tightens its strong back legs and hops away—onto the cuff, perhaps, of a man or woman walking in the street. Soon, the flea bites that person and gives him or her bubonic plague. When there are millions of infected fleas in an area, all of them hopping about from rat to rat and from rats to people, plague becomes epidemic and starts killing thousands of people.

It's important to note that oriental rat fleas themselves get sick when they become infected with bubonic plague. The effect of this on a flea is different, however, than it is on a person. Instead of developing fever, dizziness, and nausea, a flea develops a severe blockage of its digestive system.

At an advanced stage, this blockage becomes so severe that a flea can't swallow anything, not even blood it has sucked from a victim. Unfortunately, instead of simply ceasing to try to eat, infected fleas go right on hopping about and drilling holes in the skin of people and rats. Ultimately, this means that an infected flea winds up choking on a mouthful of blood while its drill-like mouth-parts are still sunk in the skin of a victim. If the blockage is serious enough, the flea will actually vomit blood back down its mouth-parts into the victim's skin. In the vomit, of course, is enough plague bacillus to set off the raging symptoms of black death.

This vomiting is a crucial link in the spread of plague from rats to people and from one person to another. To be sure, in-

Multituds flying from London by water in boats & barges.

308

Carts full of dead to bury.

fected fleas can also spread the plague when tiny drops of their saliva leak into the bite wound they make in a victim. They can also spread it by way of their feces. How?

Consider for a moment what happens when a flea bites a person. Typically, a flea defecates before, during, or right after it bites. And these feces contain deadly plague bacillus.

Now, consider what it feels like when a flea bites. Some people feel an itchy sting right away; others feel it a little later. Ultimately, almost everyone feels it strongly enough to scratch. A well-aimed scratch, of course, crushes the infected flea—feces, plague bacillus, and all—into the bite wound. The tiny bit of plague baccillus that gets into the wound this way is more than enough to send black death galloping through a person's system.

HOW EPIDEMICS DEVELOP

It would seem, with rat fleas so suited to spreading black death by way of their vomit and feces, that there would be epidemics of this disease raging constantly over the globe. It's obvious, however, that this does not happen. In fact, bubonic plague today is largely under control except in some rural areas of Asia, Africa, and South America. Now and then, small epidemics do break out and threaten to grow larger. None have, however, for years, and there are good reasons why.

One of the main things that keeps bubonic plague from spreading the way it used to is better sanitation in cities. Better

TWO SCENES FROM THE GREAT
PLAGUE OF LONDON, IN 1665.
OVER 68,000 PEOPLE DIED FROM
THE DISEASE IN THAT CITY ALONE.

sanitation means less garbage around and less for rats to eat, which in turn means fewer rats in the streets ready to act as a reservoir of plague.

During big epidemics of the past, such as the one Boccaccio witnessed in Florence, rats were very common in cities. In fact, lots of dead rats in the street have been remarked upon by many writers who suffered through plague epidemics.

If you think for a moment, it's easy to see why lots of rats are necessary to get an epidemic rolling. Let's say an infected rat scurries down the rope of a ship docked in New York. The rat runs into a nearby building and discovers a hole in the floor that leads into the city sewage system. Blocks away, the rat begins to feel the effects of bubonic plague. It lies down and dies.

Soon, the rat fleas clinging to the fur of the dead rat begin to perceive a change in their life. Biting the rat produces no more blood. And no blood to a flea means death.

At this point, if there are other rats nearby, there is a chance one or more of the fleas will succeed in hopping onto the fur of a new victim. In a modern city, however, there are simply not enough rats around for this to happen. Typically, the infected fleas from a plague-carrying rat simply die of digestive-system blockage and the disease dies with them. It's possible, of course, even in a modern city, that a few infected fleas might make a successful leap onto a new victim. It's even possible that one or more human victims might be struck down before the disease stops. Ultimately it does stop, though, because of the lack of basic material—lots and lots of rats.

WHAT IF . . .

At this point it may seem that oriental rat fleas are no longer big killers, and that perhaps they don't even belong in a book about killer insects. In terms of the number of people who currently die each year, that's probably true. But in terms of the lingering death potential, nothing could be further from the truth. Oriental rat fleas and the disease they spread still pose a considerable threat to modern cities.

The key to minimizing that threat is sanitation. A city with clean streets and good garbage collection has very few rats running about to help bubonic plague get started. A dirty city, on the other hand, has lots of rats ready to be infected by oriental rat fleas.

It's not known if a modern city could ever be hit quite the same way Florence was in 1348 or London was in 1664. One thing that would probably stop bubonic plague from becoming that bad is the development of medicines to combat it. There is no perfect cure for the plague, but some antibiotics do work quite well. Additionally, there is an injection now that people can take to reduce their chances of developing black death.

Medicines aside, bubonic plague still poses a threat in certain circumstances. If it hit a city such as New York, it would probably hit suddenly and begin causing deaths before it was discovered that thousands, even millions, of tiny oriental rat fleas were hopping from the bodies of dead rats onto the fur of live rats, or worse still, onto the cuffs of passersby or the fur of dogs being walked in the street.

Let's look at the ultimate horror story that could (but probably won't) happen. To make the story believable, imagine it taking place in New York City during a long strike by sanitation workers. . . .

Desiring changes in their working conditions, the sanitation workers have refused to pick up garbage for weeks. It's summer and the piles of refuse along the streets have begun to smell.

Worse still, the presence of so many table scraps and other edible garbage has led to an explosion of the city's rat population.

In sewer pipes beneath the streets, in abandoned buildings, and finally even in the basements of occupied buildings, thousands of rats begin to reproduce. Fattened on garbage, the sleek, long-tailed animals grow bolder and bolder. Soon, even during the day, the piles of refuse are swarming with rats. At night there are even more of the animals in the streets.

At the height of the problem, a ship pulls into New York harbor with a load of coffee from northern Brazil, where a small plague outbreak has occurred. As required by law, the skipper fastens rat guards to all the mooring lines of his ship. The round plate-shaped pieces of metal fasten over the ropes and present a barrier that rats can't cross.

That night, however, when almost everyone is asleep, a large wharf rat infected with plague bacillus scurries from beneath a pile of cargo on the main deck and looks around. Momentarily, it hops onto a railing and spots a board that someone has left leaning against the side of the ship. Its black, beady eyes alert, the rat races down the board, crosses an open, well-lit area, and ducks into the shadows.

There, at the base of a warehouse, it pauses for a moment to nip at an area of pain on its back leg where an infected oriental rat flea has just bitten. Troubled by a growing sense of nausea and discomfort, the rat quickly seeks out a hole in the building. Inside, it wriggles beneath some sacks and collapses with exhaustion.

By morning the rat is dead. But not the fleas in its fur. All of them, about 100, are very much alive.

THE ORIENTAL RAT FLEA.

That night a few of them leap onto the fur of a domestic rat drawn to the pile of sacks. At daybreak the rat slips into a nearby sewer drain and scurries away toward the heart of the city. It is now just a matter of time.

Quickly, the few infected fleas lay eggs, reproduce, and begin to scatter beneath the city by hopping from rat to rat. As they do, they spread bubonic plague in an ever wider circle.

Meanwhile, the dead, decomposing wharf rat that started the disease has been discovered by a dock worker. The worker grasps the animal by the tail and hurls it onto a pile of rubbish. As he does, one of the remaining infected fleas hops onto his hand.

Hungry for blood, the flea drills through the skin of the dockworker's hand and tries to suck itself a fresh meal. Its digestive system blocked by plague bacillus, the flea vomits into the wound instead. Death is loose in the dock worker's system.

The same is true for the city as a whole. Throughout the sewage system now, thousands of rats have died. Here and there, dead rats have begun to appear on the streets, their stomachs bloated with rot. Soon, a stench of dead animal is mingling with the smell of uncollected garbage.

Then it happens. The dock worker who tossed out the dead wharf rat becomes ill. He develops painful knots in his groin which begin to spread to other parts of his body. He becomes nauseous, feverish, and dizzy; his tongue turns brown and develops a furry feeling. His illness is diagnosed as bubonic plague, and a wave of terror washes over the city.

Health officials from all over the country fly into New York. The army is brought in to carry away all the garbage and to mount a massive rat-control plan. For many people, however, it is too late.

A few days later, hundreds of people develop the same symptoms as the dock worker. Then thousands of people become sick. Finally, people begin to die.

[20]

Despite the use of drugs, despite efforts to do away with the garbage and the rats, bubonic plague "explodes" into an epidemic. Soon, the city is eerily quiet. With tens of thousands of people sick, thousands more dead, and millions having fled to the surrounding countryside, the streets are largely empty except for soldiers and police in strange fleaproof clothing.

Is all this possible? Could it truly happen?

The answer is yes, under the right circumstances. The oriental rat flea with its ugly drill-like mouth and strong back legs is still a killer worth remembering.

Chapter 4
Bees, Wasps, and Hornets

To some people, one of the most frightening things in the world is the thought of being chased and stung by an angry swarm of bees, wasps, hornets. In sufficient doses the venom, or poison, of these insects can kill any animal on earth—an elephant, a horse, a dog, a chicken, and even a human being. Scientists tell us that stinging-insect venom is as deadly as cobra venom. Some scientists say it is twice as deadly.

Here are just a few random examples of people being killed by bees and wasps (any newspaper will provide others):

■ In 1977 a naturalist by the name of George Handlers was walking in Mount Washington State Forest in Massachusetts when he was stung by a bee. Handlers died before help arrived.

■ In 1974 an Oregon man had the misfortune to be swooped down upon by an angry bee. The bee went into his ear and stung him there, releasing enough venom to put him in shock. The man died very quickly.

■ In 1970 five people in various parts of France died from the sting of wasps, all within ten days.

The important thing about these examples is the fact that they involve a single insect, not a swarm. To understand how a single bee, wasp, or hornet can kill a person, it's necessary to know what happens when these insects sting.

As anyone who's seen a bee or wasp up close can tell you, the body of these insects is almost 8-shaped. Up front is the head and upper body. Behind that is a pinched waist, followed by the lower body. At the tip of the lower body is a stiff hairlike stinger sharp enough on the end to penetrate skin.

When threatened, bees and other stinging insects buzz rapidly toward the enemy they want to sting and more or less sit down. With amazing speed, they direct their lower body toward the skin surface and insert their stinger. At that point, muscles inside the insect pump, or squeeze, venom down the hollow inside of the stinger into the flesh of the victim.

Worker honeybees leave their stinger inside the skin of the victim and, as a result, soon die. Other stinging insects simply pull their stinger out and, if they want, sting again and again. For the victim it's worse usually to be stung by a bee that leaves its stinger behind, because muscular contractions by the stinger continue for some time after the insect has left. These contractions squirt more and more venom into the wound until the stinger stops moving on its own, or until the victim manages to get the stinger out of his or her skin.

For most people, a single sting of this sort produces a painful welt and little else. Within hours the pain and the welt are usually gone.

Other people, however, such as those described earlier, react violently to a sting and begin to itch all over. This can be followed

by a general swelling of the body, nausea, dizziness, stomach pain, and tightness in the chest. Occasionally this kind of reaction leads to slurring of speech, weakness, a fall in blood pressure, and even coma. In extreme cases, death follows within an hour or two, or as long after the sting as ten days.

This reaction to an insect sting is what doctors call *anaphylactic shock*. It is similar to the reaction some people have to penicillin and a few other drugs. Why do some people have this reaction to a single sting while others have no reaction, even after four, five, or more stings? Exactly what in the bee and wasp venom causes this reaction?

Doctors aren't absolutely certain how to answer either of these questions. The venom of these insects is known to contain some powerful substances, at least two of which are helpful to people. A substance called apamin, for instance, restores normal heart rhythm when injected into the blood. Another substance helps relieve the pain of arthritis.

Ultimately, the venom of these insects is best thought of as a poison that has a bigger effect on some people than it does on others. Remember: Even people who do not get anaphylactic shock die when exposed to enough of this venom.

GOOD GUYS/BAD GUYS

Some stinging insects are quiet, peace-loving creatures that like nothing better than to be left alone. Others are mean-tempered and quick to attack. Still others are slow to attack but, once angered, are dogged in pursuit. An example of the latter is a large, dark-bodied wasp commonly called the black wasp. Sufficiently

THE TARANTULA HAWK WASP.

[25]

angered, this insect has been known to chase an enemy hundreds of yards, swooping and diving about like a fighter plane. Larger than most wasps, the black wasp releases a lot of venom when it stings.

A type of wasp, known in areas where it is most plentiful as the yellow jacket, is a good example of a stinging insect that's quick to attack when disturbed. Unfortunately, these insects have a habit of building their nests in places where people can run into them. One good place to look for a yellow jacket nest is in a tin can left on the ground in a weedy, brushy area. Another good place to look for one is under the eaves of a shed, or even under a bird feeder.

Which of the stinging insects are peace-loving? The bumblebee is, and so is the honeybee to some extent. Both of these insects do sting people quite often, however, largely because their habit of buzzing about from flower to flower tends to bring them in contact with people. Bees and people clash most often when bees are visiting flowers such as clover that bloom near the ground. A typical way for someone to get stung by a bee is to step on one barefoot, or sit down on one. Occasionally people also get stung by sniffing at a flower that has a bee inside of it.

It's rare, but people also get stung by disturbing a beehive, unaware that bees live inside. Those who do this often get stung many times because bees, like most animals, react violently to having their home disturbed.

A STING FROM A HORNET MAY CAUSE
SEVERE PROBLEMS FOR SOME PEOPLE,
BUT FOR MOST IT WILL CAUSE ONLY A
WELT AND A BIT OF PAIN.

MASS ATTACKS

The thought of someone being stung many times brings up the subject of mass attacks. It is the possibility of such an attack that frightens people most. There is good reason for the fear, because a mass attack by bees, wasps, or hornets can result in death for even the healthiest person, and particularly a child. Someone attacked this way need not be allergic to stings to die from them, either. In large doses, bee venom kills just like any other poison.

To be sure, people rarely provoke a mass bee attack by simply walking up to a beehive. On the contrary, most mass attacks are caused accidentally. Here are a few ways mass attacks occur:

■ A man tries to cut down a tree for firewood, unaware it is hollow and filled with wild honeybees. At the first cut hundreds of bees pour out of a hole.

■ A woman stoops to enter a little-used tool shed and straightens up just inside. Her head bumps against a nest of black wasps, exciting them to attack instantly.

■ A man walking in the woods pushes a limb aside, unaware that a big gray hornet's nest is attached to it, hidden by some leaves. The nest falls to the ground, and hornets fly up seeking the enemy who has upset their lives.

■ A man cleaning up a patch of weeds bends over to pick up a rusty coffee can. As he lifts it, dozens of yellow jackets emerge, angered that their nest had been disturbed.

THE YELLOW JACKET, NAMED
FOR THE ALTERNATING
YELLOW AND BLACK BANDS
AROUND ITS ABDOMEN.

[29]

MASS COMMUNICATION

Anyone can think of other ways a mass attack might be provoked. What is particularly interesting, however, is the way stinging insects manage to communicate their alarm to one another quickly enough for a mass attack to occur. Insects, of course, can't shout instructions to one another. What stinging insects can do, however, is produce a chemical when they grow alarmed or angry.

This chemical, called an alarm pheremone, has a special smell or quality that other insects of the same species react to instantly. It's not known with absolute certainty how stinging insects smell this chemical in the air. However they smell it, the presence of a tiny bit of alarm pheremone—even the small amount given off by a single bee—is enough at times to alert and anger an entire swarm of stinging insects.

As strange as this chemical communication sounds, it is thought to be responsible for the varying attack behavior of stinging insects. Mean-tempered insects such as yellow jackets, for example, are thought to produce a lot of this chemical when they grow angry or alarmed. Ordinary honeybees, on the other hand, are thought to give off very little.

It's fortunate that honeybees are slow to anger because they tend to live in much larger groups than, say, wasps. A typical wasp's nest might hold 100 or so wasps. A beehive, though, can hold tens of thousands of bees, and apiaries (places where a lot of beehives are kept together) can hold millions of bees—so many that the humming of their wings can be heard quite a distance away.

A WASP'S NEST.

[30]

What would an apiary be like if honeybees gave off a lot of alarm pheremone and were quick to attack in swarms? There's no need to guess actually, because there are apiaries of that sort in South America full of bees so quick to attack that they have been called killer bees. In many ways, these are truly fearsome insects.

Chapter 5
Killer Bees

The insect that has come to be known as the killer bee is actually an ordinary African honeybee that has been moved from its home in Africa to a new home in South America. Their reputation for being killers comes from their remarkable tendency to attack without much reason and to sting an enemy until it dies.

Here are just a few things these insects have done in recent years:

■   In September 1965, a swarm of killer bees invaded Rio de Janeiro, a large coastal city in Brazil. They gathered in front of the Armed Forces Military Command and began attacking people. Their attacks became so vicious that soldiers on guard duty had to run away.

■   In June of that same year, a resident of Caieiras, near São Paulo, tried to burn a hive of killer bees out of the chimney of a bar. According to *Time* magazine, the bees "rose in a buzzing mass that darkened the sky and swarmed into the bar where they stung a wine salesman senseless and left so many stings in the bald dome of the bartender that he thought he was growing hair again." Before the bees moved out of the area, they stung 500 people, and then they buzzed off across nearby farms where they left behind flocks of dead chickens, a dozen writhing dogs, and two horses so badly stung they could not eat for days.

Reports say that scores of people every year have been killed by these bees in Brazil and in other South American countries. Literally thousands of animals—dogs, cats, cows, and others —have died after wandering into killer bee's nests.

The problem with killer bees is not that they have more venom than other bees, but that they are simply bad tempered. Instead of attacking singly, or in twos or threes, they attack in swarms and usually don't stop stinging until their victim is dead or under cover. Often, these attacks occur with little or no warning.

In the early 1970s, when killer bee reports first began to come out of South America, a group of scientists went down to Brazil to study them and see how big a problem they truly were. One of the tests the scientists made on killer bees was designed to see how many times a hive full of bees would sting a piece of leather dangled in front of their home.

To alert the bees and start the test, the researcher jostled the hive with his hand. Instantly, killer bees swarmed out of the hive and began attacking. They stung the piece of leather swaying near their door an astounding ninety-two times in five seconds,

WILD HONEYBEES SWARMING
TO BUILD A NEW HIVE.

nearly twice the number of times it would take to kill an average person.

The reaction of the bees was so frightening that the scientist turned to leave the area immediately instead of waiting the thirty seconds the test required. The bees began to attack the scientist (fortunately, he was wearing protective clothing) and chased him for more than a mile.

Killer bees have other habits that make them dangerous to people and animals. For one thing, they don't stay in their hive or their original home area the way ordinary honeybees usually do. Instead, they seem to grow tired of an area quite often, and simply leave in a great swarm. At such times they are at their worst. Threatened at all, even accidentally by a cow in a field, say, or by a person walking down a street, they rush to attack and sting as many times as they can.

Another dangerous thing about killer bees is their tendency to live in small burrows, empty boxes, tin cans, and even cracks in a building—all places where people and animals are likely to disturb them. Worse still, a swarm of killer bees tends to reproduce very fast and split off into new swarms that can soon infest an entire area. An area infested this way with killer bees is a little like a military minefield. A person or animal walking through such an area sets off a swarm and begins to run, only to step into another killer bee burrow and set off a second swarm. Soon, with so many bees alerted and giving off alarm pheremone, the entire field or yard full of bees goes on the rampage and begins to sting anything that moves. Many deaths due to killer bees have been caused just this way.

A good indication of the speed with which killer bees reproduce and infest an area is their short history in Brazil. Life began for the killer bee in Brazil in 1957 when twenty-six queen bees were accidentally released. Seventeen years later, in 1974, those twenty-six queens had multiplied into millions and had spread over an area almost as big as the United States. Today, there are even more killer bees than that, and they cover a much wider area.

A population explosion like this is common when any kind of animal is moved from one part of the world to another. Rabbits, for example, when they were brought to Australia, soon multiplied so fast they became a menace to crops.

What the killer bee and the rabbit have in common is fewer natural enemies in their new home than they had in their old home. This means they have an ability to reproduce offspring that is greater than is needed to keep their species alive and well. Scientists call this kind of situation an imbalance of nature. In the case of the killer bee, the imbalance is a dangerous one that might have become even more dangerous if the bees had spread into a country like the United States.

Killer bees were brought into Brazil by Warwick Kerr, a bee expert who wanted to create a bee that worked harder and produced more honey than the bees that were already in that country. His idea was to cross the two strains of bees—the nasty but hard-working Africans and the docile but less-productive bees already there—and come up with a new bee that combined the best qualities of both. It was a good idea, but a lot of things went wrong.

When Warwick Kerr went to Africa looking for African bees, he knew these insects were possibly too aggressive to be moved into an area such as Brazil where their natural enemies were lacking. For that reason, he sought out the gentlest Africans he could find and he released or destroyed those that seemed to be bad-tempered.

Months later, he narrowed his choice down to fifty gentle queen bees, which he shipped to Portugal. It was there in the city of Lisbon, while the bees were waiting to be shipped on to Brazil, that the first thing went wrong.

A customs official happened to go into the warehouse where the bees were stored, and he heard them buzzing about in their box. He ordered them all killed, unaware that Warwick Kerr had permission from the government to take the bees back to Brazil.

When Kerr, who was still in Africa, heard about his bees being destroyed, he looked for some more so he wouldn't have to go home empty-handed. In a hurry this time, he rounded up 150 of the first queen bees he could find, making almost no effort to weed out mean bees.

Back in Brazil, Kerr put fifty-six of these bees into an experimental apiary. As a precaution, he equipped his hives with excluders, special devices that kept the queens from leaving. His long-range plan was to cross the African queens with bees that were already in Brazil, and then do away with the possibly dangerous Africans. Unfortunately, this is when something else went wrong.

A worker in the apiary, unaware of the danger of the Africans, left the excluder off some of the hives one day. Almost immediately, 26 of the African bees escaped.

At first the impact of the bees was thought to be good. The new breed of bee that developed locally with the introduction of the Africans produced far more honey than the beekeepers had ever seen. All of them were happy with the Africans, and they fought Warwick Kerr's efforts to stop the bees from spreading. By the time the true danger of the bees was known it was too late. The killer bee was in South America for good. In the African countryside, where their numbers were controlled by many natural enemies, killer bees were no problem. It was only when they were

MOST HONEYBEES ARE PEACE-LOVING
INSECTS, BUT THEY WILL STING IF
THEY OR THEIR NEST IS DISTURBED.

moved into an area with fewer natural enemies and crowded with people and animals that the trouble started.

WHAT IF . . .

What would happen if these same insects made their way to a more populous and busy country than Brazil? To France, for example, to Spain, or to the United States?

Some scientists are concerned about that possibility. With so many killer bees flying about in Brazil, it's possible that some bees might eventually swarm quietly aboard a ship and stay there until they arrive in another country. It's also possible that bee-keepers will smuggle some of these bees out of Brazil because of their hardworking habits. The most likely possibility of all is that killer bees will eventually reach new homes by expanding their range a few miles each year. The country most worried about this possibility is the United States. One need only look at a map to see why.

North and South America are connected by a sliver of land called the Isthmus of Panama. Eventually, if killer bees keep spreading, it's almost certain that they will infest this sliver of land and move across the Panama Canal, across Central America and Mexico, and finally across the border into the southwestern United States.

A few years ago, scientists were convinced this was going to happen very soon and that serious trouble was going to result. There were predictions that many Americans would die from bee stings. Great damage to cattle and horses was also forecast.

It was during this time when scientists were forecasting problems with the killer bee in the United States that Arthur Herzog wrote a fantasy book about the bees that was made into a movie. The book and movie depicted huge cloudlike swarms of killer bees sweeping across the country, forcing people to stay in their homes and eventually bringing business and everything else to a halt.

Since the book and movie appeared, scientists have looked again at the killer bee situation and seen a couple of new developments. For one thing, the bees have been slowed down in their movement toward the United States by the damp climate of the Amazon jungle. To get around this huge jungle, the bees have begun to move slowly along the coast of Brazil, a few miles a year. If they finally arrive in the United States (and no one is as certain of that as they used to be), it will take far longer than was previously thought.

In the meantime, killer bees in some parts of Brazil have begun to quiet down. It appears, at least in some places, that the bee Warwick Kerr wanted to create in experimental apiaries is being created naturally in the wild. Because of matings between African and local bees, a hardworking but not-so-nasty bee is beginning to emerge.

This is not true, however, in all parts of Brazil. There are still many millions of truly bad-tempered killer bees that explode with anger and alarm at the least disturbance. Obviously, the killer bee is far from being a minor threat. Among killer insects, it is one of the most interesting and important.

Chapter 6
Tsetse Flies

The third great killer among insects is a small harmless-looking fly that resembles an ordinary housefly. Called "tsetse" because of the sound its wings make in the air, this insect lives only in Africa. It kills an estimated 7,000 people a year there and makes countless others very sick. It bites humans and animals, giving them a terrible disease called sleeping sickness.

What people refer to as the tsetse is actually an entire group of bloodsucking flies. In all, there are more than twenty species of these flies, some of which are more comfortable in a jungle and some of which are more suited for dry, savanna-type country. Together, these insects have kept people from developing a chunk of Africa measuring 4,000,000 square miles (10,360,000 sq km). That's more land than is found in the entire United States.

A tsetse fly is just slightly larger than a housefly. It has the same number of legs as a housefly (or any insect), and its wings work much like a housefly's, too. A little closer look, however, reveals some differences. For one thing, tsetse flies aren't black like houseflies, but yellowish to dark brown. Tsetse flies also differ in the way they come to rest on a person or thing. Unlike the housefly, the tsetse overlaps its wings when it is not flying.

When you look still more closely, the major difference between the flies becomes obvious. The mouthparts of the housefly might be considered ugly, but those of the tsetse fly are awesome-looking. They extend forward from its head a little like a bayonet. This bladelike projection is rounded at the base and enclosed in a protective sheath.

When a tsetse wants to bite and suck blood from a person or animal, it lands on the skin, quickly folds its wings, and lowers its "bayonet" to the skin's surface. Then it simply nods its head sharply and rams the bayonet into the victim's skin. As it does, the sheath around the bayonet spreads outward across the skin. Hurriedly, the fly sucks in its meal of blood and flies away. Typically, all of this happens so fast that the victim does not have time to fight back.

As with the oriental rat flea, it is not the bite of the tsetse fly that matters very much. The pain a tsetse fly causes by taking some blood is minor. And so is the wound that develops where its bayonet went in. What isn't minor is the contamination a tsetse fly can cause.

The organisms that tsetse flies can contaminate people with are called *trypanosomes.* Small, roundish particles of life with a tail on one end, trypanosomes are very harmful to the human body. If not stopped, they multiply inside most people and eventually kill them.

THE TSETSE FLY INSERTS ITS
"BAYONET" INTO A MAN'S ARM.

NOTE, AFTER THE MEAL, HOW ITS
ABDOMEN IS SWOLLEN WITH BLOOD.

HOW THE DISEASE SPREADS

There are two basic ways that a tsetse fly spreads trypanosomes. The first way involves both humans and animals, and it involves a very deadly type of trypanosome called *Trypanosome rhodesiense.*

These tiny trypanosomes move about inside the bloodstream of any one of several African animals, particularly antelopes. Unlike plague bacillus, which kills the rat that carries it, trypanosomes don't hurt wild animals, though they do hurt domestic animals such as cows. Interestingly, trypanosomes don't hurt tsetse flies either. When these insects become infected by swooping down on an antelope, say, and taking in a meal of contaminated blood, the trypanosomes invade the digestive system of the tsetse and begin to develop and multiply. In about a month—eighteen to thirty-four days generally—the fully mature trypanosomes move from the tsetse's digestive system to its salivary glands.

At this point, the trypanosomes are like a deadly poison in the tsetse's mouth. To infect a person, a tsetse fly needs only a quick touchdown and a jab with its bayonet, and the deed is done.

It takes so few trypanosomes to infect a person that a tsetse fly need not vomit into the bite wound the way an oriental rat flea does. In fact, a tsetse fly need not even feed on a person's blood to give him or her sleeping sickness. A man can see a tsetse fly on his arm, for example, and immediately slap it away. But if the tsetse's bayonet has broken the skin and a tiny bit of saliva has rubbed off the tsetse's mouthparts into the bite wound, it is more than enough to cause sleeping sickness.

The second way that tsetse flies spread disease is simply by taking in a deadly load of trypanosomes from one person and giving it to another person. Either of the two types of trypanosomes that cause sleeping sickness can be spread this way, but most often it is *Trypanosome gambiense.* A slower, less-certain killer than *Trypanosome rhodesiense,* it is rarely found in the bloodstream of wild animals.

People themselves, then, are the major reservoir of this type of sleeping sickness. To keep it going, tsetse flies simply fly about in a community biting sick people and then, after the necessary passage of time, biting a person who is well.

There is yet a third way that tsetse flies spread sleeping sickness around. You might say they "track trypanosomes" into a human being the way a person tracks mud into a house. In other words, when a tsetse fly bites an infected animal or person his mouthparts become soaked with contaminated blood. For up to two days, this blood contains enough trypanosomes, alive and vigorous, to spread sleeping sickness directly.

Trypanosomes spread this way don't have to make the round-about journey through the tsetse fly's digestive system and then back to his salivary glands. They are, instead, simply "tracked" from one person to another. In areas such as the Congo where sleeping sickness is very common, a lot of tsetse flies buzz about all the time, their mouthparts soaked with contaminated blood.

THE EFFECTS

The effects of trypanosomes on a human being are gradual but still devastating in the end. Typically, trypanosomes simply swim about in the bloodstream of a person for quite a while at first, multiplying and gathering strength. This incubation period, as it is called, lasts from ten days to three weeks or longer, up to as long as five years.

After this stage is over, the rapidly multiplying trypanosomes enter the lymph glands and finally the nervous system. In the early stage, when trypanosomes are just beginning to enter the lymph system, a person suffers only a slight fever and maybe some swelling in the lymph glands. After that, the symptoms grow worse. The mild fever creeps higher, particularly in the afternoons, and is accompanied by general pain, fast pulse, and even more swelling of the lymph glands.

When trypanosomes begin their invasion of the nervous system, the symptoms of this disease grow truly alarming. A person's fingers and tongue often start to tremble, and it's not unusual for hallucinations to occur. Gradually, this stage of the disease leads to hysteria and an extremely excited state called mania.

After this stage passes, the symptoms suddenly reverse. A person becomes sad and lazy, unable to speak above a low murmur. Walking becomes slow and difficult, and the victim becomes very thin, almost skeletonlike. This is followed by a tendency to sleep at odd hours and, finally, by an inability to wake up again. Ultimately, a person with sleeping sickness dies.

The suffering and death that the tsetse fly causes among people obviously qualify it as one of the great killers. Actually, the tsetse is a great killer of domestic animals, too, particularly cattle.

Over and over, in some parts of Africa, people have tried to clear the jungle, plant pastures, and raise cattle, only to find that all of the cows have died of sleeping sickness. It's in this way, as a killer of livestock, that the tsetse fly has succeeded best at keeping people from developing parts of Africa.

As you might expect, people have tried to fight this insect and remove it from the countryside. These efforts, most of which have failed, have cost huge amounts of money and in some cases have damaged the environment. Mass spraying with DDT and other strong pesticides, for example, has killed some forms of wildlife and wiped out other, helpful insects.

Instead of fighting tsetse flies directly, some people have focused their attention on sleeping sickness and tried to stamp it out by removing the wild animals that provide a reservoir for trypanosomes. Without infected animals around, it was thought that tsetse flies would soon be harmless. People who believed this, killed thousands of antelopes and other deerlike animals, only to discover that small ratlike animals—far too numerous ever to get rid of—were also a reservoir of trypanosomes. The killing of antelope did no good at all.

It may sound strange, but some people say that the tsetse fly is actually a good insect to have in Africa. They point out that tsetse flies are most numerous in those areas where African wildlife is richest. This means that the tsetse fly, by keeping people away, is protecting the wildlife's land from developers who would turn it into croplands and pastures.

There may be some truth to this view of the tsetse fly. But what about the people who die each year after suffering all the symptoms of sleeping sickness? And what about all the people in Africa who could live better if cattle were grown on land being "protected" by the tsetse?

Such questions are being debated now. How they are answered will probably determine how much money is spent fighting the tsetse. If enough is spent, perhaps one day the tsetse will no longer be an important killer. For the present, however, it is.

Chapter 7
Mosquitoes

The fourth great killer among insects is one that almost everyone has seen and, more than likely, has even been bitten by. Called mosquito after the Spanish word for "little fly" (*mosca-ito*), this insect is as well known by people living in the suburbs of New York City as it is by Indians living in the jungles of South America. Even Eskimos in Alaska know it and dread its appearance each spring.

Though all mosquitoes look very much alike to the naked eye, there are great differences among the various species. In all, there are about 3,000 different kinds of mosquitoes. Some have long, wispy legs and small bodies, while others are fatter, chunkier, and ungraceful. Some are very tiny, others about the size of a dime.

The mosquito, like the oriental rat flea and the tsetse fly, kills largely by spreading disease. Its bite alone does not threaten the average person's life. A faint jab of pain followed by itching is the typical result of a mosquito bite. Later, a small red welt usually appears on the skin where the mosquito bit.

While most of their damage is done by spreading disease, their bite alone can be harmful. In sufficient numbers, the bites of mosquitoes have occasionally made people sick and even killed them or driven them crazy. Animals, too, particularly in the Far North, have been known to run wildly through the forest and even pitch themselves off cliffs to escape clouds of hungry, bloodsucking mosquitoes.

The artist John Groth, recalling a trip to Lapland, described an encounter he had with mosquitoes this way:

> I was fishing alone one afternoon quite a distance from camp when, suddenly, mosquitos began to swarm up from the grass and shrubs and blanket me with their bodies. Soon, there were so many mosquitos on my white fishing hat that it looked black. . . . When the mosquitos started to bite me, I had to run away. I think they would have bitten me to death if I hadn't fled.

There is yet another way that mosquitoes are occasionally dangerous, and this is when their bites set off an acute allergic reaction in a person's body. This, however, happens very rarely.

Far more important is the bloodsucking nature of the mosquito that drives it to fly about almost constantly in search of animals and people to feed upon. In parts of the world where diseases are rampant, the blood hunger of the mosquito makes it a very effective carrier of certain illnesses. Two of the most common diseases that mosquitoes spread are malaria and yellow fever.

ONLY FEMALES

Interestingly, it is only the female mosquito that bites people and spreads disease. The male, unequipped to bite through flesh, feeds mostly on the tiny amounts of sweet fluid that it can suck from flowers. Females also feed on flowers at times, though they must have human or animal blood to produce eggs that will hatch.

The time of day that a mosquito's hunger for blood is greatest depends on the species. Some species are hungriest at daybreak, while others feel the greatest hunger after dark and on through the night until just before sunrise.

No matter when they go in search of blood, female mosquitoes seem to be able to track victims down by smelling them from a great distance. Smell also seems to be a trigger of sorts that makes a mosquito bite and take in some blood. To prove this, some scientists had a person place a hand on a pane of glass. The pane of glass was then placed in a cage of hungry female mosquitoes.

Instantly, the mosquitoes in the cage descended on the pane of glass and began to probe it with their needlelike mouths, trying to suck blood from it. Some of the mosquitoes in the cage continued to probe the glass for as long as a half-hour, at which time the human scent on the glass had gone away.

Smell, then, appears to be what draws a mosquito toward an animal or person. Oddly, though, a mosquito doesn't usually streak toward a victim in a straight line the way an angry wasp, for example, usually does. Instead, a mosquito tends to approach a victim indirectly, hesitantly. Even in a small room, mosquitoes have been observed to fly about for a minute or more before touching down lightly on a victim. Perhaps you have seen

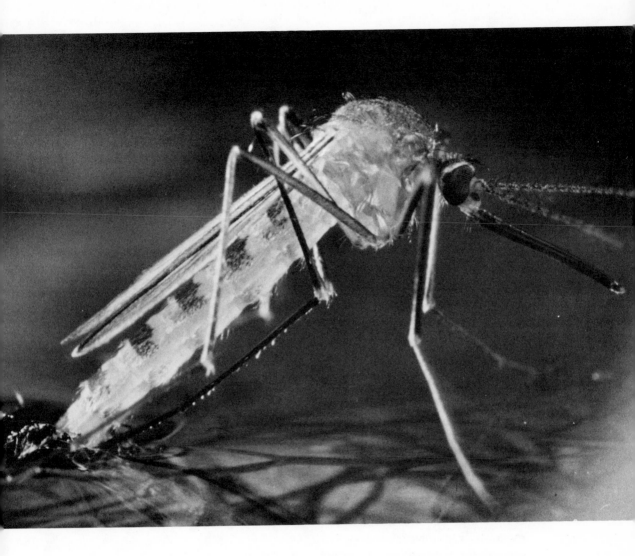

A COMMON FEMALE MOSQUITO, HAVING JUST
EMERGED FROM ITS LARVAL STATE.

mosquitoes act this way yourself, or heard them whining about in the dark, first near, then far away, and finally near again before settling down to bite.

When a mosquito finally does touch down on a victim, it typically dawdles a while before attempting to bite. The reason for this hesitation is unclear, but it's thought that a mosquito has some type of sensory organs in its feet. Before biting, it more or less "smells with its feet" for a while by walking around.

Ultimately, if the mosquito has landed on a living animal or person, and if it is hungry, it will lower its mouthparts to the surface of the victim's skin. Apparently round and needlelike, these mouthparts are actually composed of five slender blades and an enclosing cover. In effect, a hungry mosquito jabs a tiny hole in its victim and then drinks the blood through the hole it has made. This jabbing through the flesh (it takes about a minute) is what makes a mosquito bite hurt.

What makes a mosquito bite itch is another matter entirely. To understand this, it's necessary to realize that the mouthparts of a mosquito are hollow. Inside the mouthparts is a tube that allows blood to go up from the bite hole into the mosquito's stomach and another tube that allows saliva to go down from the mosquito into the bite wound.

The saliva that a mosquito injects into the bite hole is thought to contain, among other things, an anticoagulant. An anticoagulant is a substance that keeps blood from clotting. This is very useful to a mosquito. Without it, a victim's blood might simply clot up and become too solid to be sucked down into a mosquito's stomach.

Some researchers think it is the irritating effect of this anticoagulant that makes a mosquito bite itch. Even more interesting is the way the excretion of saliva, whether it contains anticoagulant or not, makes mosquitoes such perfect pipelines of disease. In a way, this tendency to excrete saliva is a little like the oriental rat flea's tendency to vomit into a bite wound. Both actions insure that a disease-causing organism taken from the bloodstream of one victim gets into the bloodstream of another.

And all of this brings us back to the major diseases that mosquitoes spread: malaria and yellow fever. Let's look at malaria first.

MALARIA

This disease has been called the "worst scourge to mankind." There is good reason for this.

As recently as 1974, it was estimated that more than 100 million people in the world were suffering from malaria.

It's not known with any kind of certainty how many people die from malaria each year, but it's generally agreed that more people die from it than from any other transmittable disease. A rough estimate of the deaths would be somewhere around a million each year.

Most of the cases of malaria occur in the forested parts of Asia, Africa, Central and South America, and southern Europe. At one time, malaria was a big problem in Mississippi, Louisiana, and several other southern American states. But not any more. Today, malaria has been largely done away with in the United States, though there is no assurance that it won't make a comeback someday.

The symptoms of this disease are perhaps less spectacular than the symptoms of sleeping sickness, but they are still dramatic. The most striking symptom is the onset of fever and terrible chills. Here is the way one writer described a malaria ward in

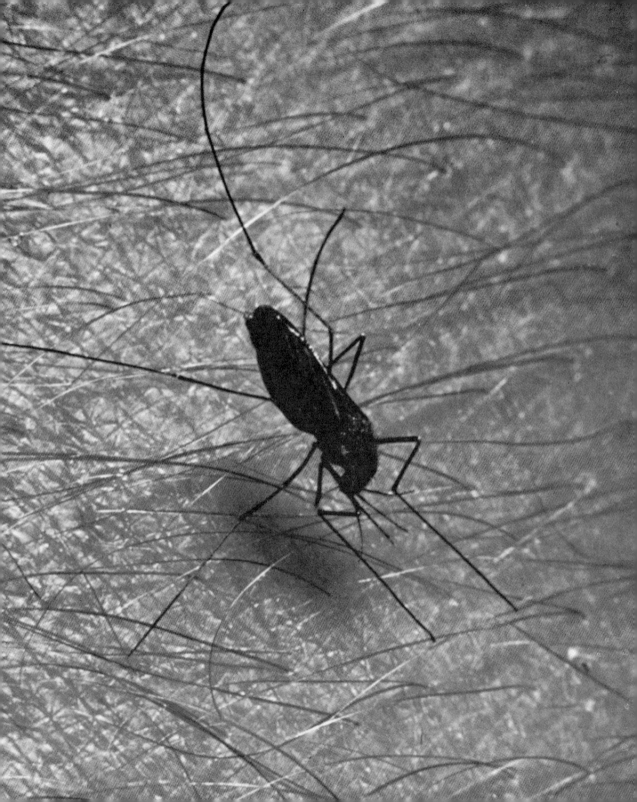

Panama City during the building of the Panama Canal:

> Often the shivering of patients in a malaria ward would be so violent the room could actually be felt to tremble; a single bed would move on the floor.

> The chills would be followed by high fever and a burning thirst. As the fever fell off, the patient would break out in a drenching sweat. For those who survived, the experience was unforgettable. With the passing of the fever, the patient was left feeling totally debilitated, mentally as well as physically. Acute depression usually set in, the "melancholia" that was so well known in Panama.

The fight to stamp out this disease has been one of the great medical struggles of all times. The first step was to discover that it was spread by mosquitoes. Before that was known, malaria was considered to be something like a bad cold one caught from swampy "bad air." (The Italian words for "bad air" are *mala aria*.)

It took the British physician, Ronald Ross, to see that the underlying connection between malaria and "bad air" was the presence of mosquitoes in swamps. At the time Ross discovered this, malaria was a huge killer raging out of control in many parts of the world, particularly in countries near the equator. The same year he matched up malaria-causing cells in the blood of a sick person with identical cells in the saliva of a particular type of mosquito, malaria killed an estimated one million people in India alone.

THE MAJOR TRANSMITTER OF MALARIA—
THE *ANOPHELES* MOSQUITO.

But it was years before lives were saved as a result of his discovery. Why? Because it was discovered that the only way to stamp out malaria was to do away with all the mosquitoes in an area that were spreading the disease from animals to humans. That was hard (and still is) because the mosquito responsible for malaria—called the *Anopheles* mosquito—lays its eggs almost anywhere. It lays them in stagnant swamps, for example, in marshes, clogged drains, ditches, and even in mud puddles.

A single Anopheles mosquito, it was further learned, can lay as many as fifty eggs a day for nearly a month. These eggs hatch in about a day. About two weeks after that, adults emerge and begin to mate almost immediately. One mosquito, then, in a single lifetime could have up to 1,000 offspring, which in turn could have tens of thousands of offspring, which could have millions, and so on.

The greatest battle against malaria and the *Anopheles* mosquito took place in the early 1900s when the Panama Canal was being built. Because the biggest battle against yellow fever also took place there, it's best to look at the two battles together. First, though, a word about yellow fever itself.

YELLOW FEVER

This disease, named for one of its major symptoms (a yellowing of the skin and eyes), is thought to have originated in West Africa. It spread from there and touched off epidemics in many parts of the world when sailing ships began to sail the world's seas for the first time.

A YELLOW FEVER PATIENT IN A HOSPITAL IN CUBA IN 1898.

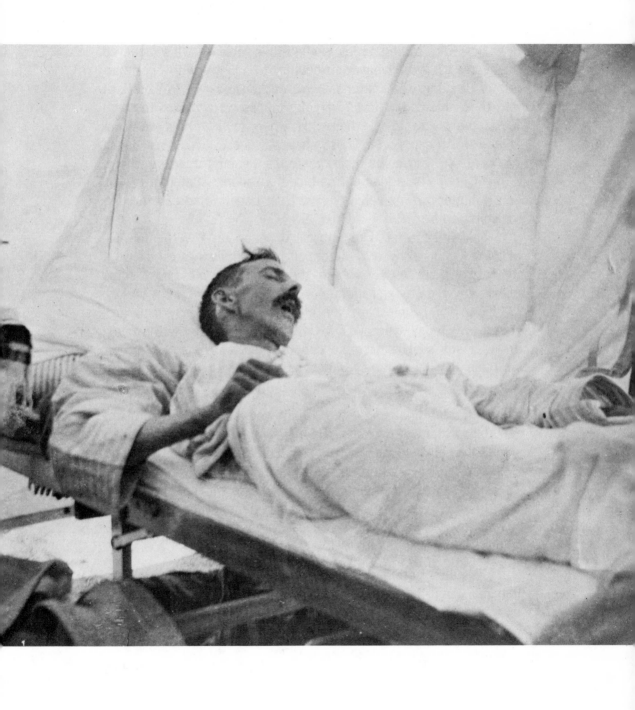

How did sailing ships spread this disease? It's believed they spread it by moving from country to country with open barrels of drinking water stored below deck. Unknown to sailors at that time, infected yellow fever mosquitoes were drawn to these barrels as places to lay their eggs when sailing ships were anchored in African ports. These stowaway mosquitoes reproduced on board ship and made their way to the sleeping quarters where, at night, they would feed on the blood of sailors. After that, it was only a matter of time before yellow fever began to spread through the ship's entire crew.

Ships that suffered an outbreak of yellow fever were often forbidden to land—anywhere. At gunpoint sometimes these ships were forced back out to sea where they soon became ghost ships manned by a few dying sailors.

The fear people had then of yellow fever is easy to understand. Even today, when yellow fever has been controlled in many areas, it still strikes terror in people's hearts. The following description by James Stanley Gilbert of what happens to people with yellow fever should give you some idea why:

> In the terminal stages the patient would spit up mouthfuls of blood—the infamous, terrifying *vomito negro,* black vomit. The end would usually come swiftly after that. The body temperature would drop, the pulse fade. The flesh would become cold to the touch—almost as cold as stone. Then, as a rule, in about eight to ten hours, the patient would die. And so great was the terror the disease generated that its victims were buried with all possible speed.

This description, from a book about the building of the Panama Canal, leaves out many yellow fever symptoms such as profound headaches ("Iron bands will clamp your brow," is the way one writer described the pain), a bad taste in the mouth ("curdled cream" one writer called it), and delirium. Gilbert himself likened this delirium to a heaviness of the head:

Your head will weigh a ton or more
And 40 gales within it roar!

The mosquito responsible for all this horror and suffering is ironically one of the most beautiful of all mosquitoes. When not in flight, it moves about with the grace of a ballet dancer on six long, jointed legs. Its grayish tone is enlivened by a tigerlike series of silvery white stripes on its legs and throat.

The *Aedes aegypti,* as this mosquito is called, spreads yellow fever the same way the *Anopheles* mosquito spreads malaria. It bites an infected animal, becomes infected itself, and then bites a human being. In the course of biting a human, it injects saliva into the bite wound that contains yellow fever virus. But for many years, doctors thought yellow fever and malaria were both communicable diseases that began with the breathing in of bad air and then spread from person to person much like a cold.

A famous experiment during the time of the building of the Panama Canal put this belief to rest and paved the way to realizing that mosquitoes were the culprit. The experiment involved three volunteers who agreed to stay for twenty days in a one-room shack where dying yellow fever patients had been housed. For nearly a month, the volunteers slept in the dirty pajamas of yellow fever victims, on their filthy sheets that reeked of black vomit. Significantly, not one of the volunteers got yellow fever.

With other research already pointing toward *Aedes aegypti* mosquitoes as the cause of yellow fever, many people accepted this as fact. Among the people who accepted it was William Gorgas, an Army doctor who began shortly afterward his famous battle to eliminate both *Aedes aegypti* and *Anopheles* mosquitoes from Panama.

THE GREAT MOSQUITO WAR

When Gorgas arrived in that hot and steamy part of the world, the digging of the canal, which was to link the Atlantic and Pacific oceans, was very far from completion. In fact, there were growing worries that the Americans would, like the French before them, have to give up on the project and go home in defeat. One of the things holding up the canal was sickness, primarily yellow fever and malaria.

Gorgas, aware these diseases were spread by mosquitoes, was appalled at just how many of these insects there were. They seemed to be everywhere—in camps where workers lived, in the jungle, in the streets of major towns and, unbelievably, even in hospital rooms where people were already dying of yellow fever and malaria.

There were so many mosquitoes largely because people unknowingly allowed them plenty of places to lay their eggs. Heavy machinery, for example, was allowed to gouge the earth and makes holes that later filled with rainwater. Most people, just outside their door, had an open barrel which they used to collect drinking water. Worse still were the open dumps where rain-filled tin cans, old buckets, jars, and bottles were allowed to collect.

Everywhere Gorgas looked, it seemed, were egg-laying spots for mosquitoes. Most of these spots were alive with tiny wormlike creatures—wigglers, as they were called locally—which Gorgas rec-

THE *AEDES AEGYPTI* MOSQUITO,
THE CULPRIT IN THE
SPREAD OF YELLOW FEVER.

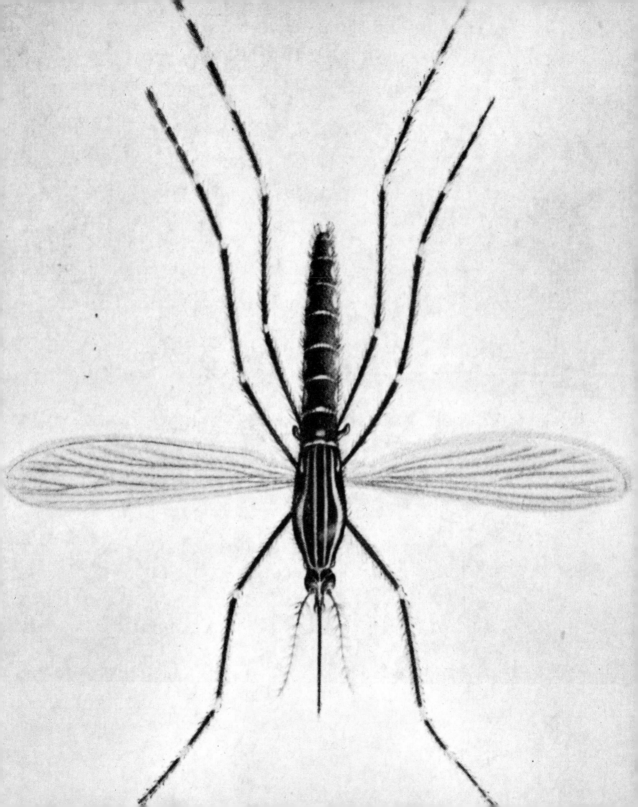

ognized to be mosquito larvae. Gorgas spotted wigglers in such odd places as a fount of holy water in front of a Catholic church and in pans of water used around plants on hospital grounds to keep ants away. Similar pans, used in hospital rooms to keep ants from crawling up on beds, also were filled with mosquito larvae.

As mentioned earlier, Gorgas attacked this huge swarm of mosquitoes by seeking to do away with all the available egg-laying spots. He started with the egg-laying spots used by yellow fever mosquitoes.

Why?

For one thing, yellow fever was the disease that was frightening workers most in Panama. Each time an outbreak of this disease occurred, there were protests by workers and threats to leave the country. At one point, an outbreak of yellow fever—accompanied by a few cases of bubonic plague—created such panic that large numbers of workers actually left on ships and refused to come back.

Another reason Gorgas attacked yellow fever mosquitoes first was because, in some ways, they were an easier target. Unlike malaria mosquitos, yellow fever mosquitoes don't use natural places such as mud puddles and stagnant pools to lay their eggs. Instead, they use only water that is in some kind of container—for example, a barrel, a tin can, or a bucket. It was therefore far easier for Gorgas to drain all these containers than it was for him to drain the thousands of natural spots that dotted all parts of the Panamanian countryside.

A PHOTOGRAPH TAKEN IN 1904
DURING THE BUILDING OF THE
PANAMA CANAL. NOTE THE POOL
OF WATER IN THE FOREGROUND.

To accomplish his goal, Gorgas enlisted a large crew of men and gave them the authority to drain or cover all containers in areas where people lived. Also, where a case of yellow fever broke out, he immediately sent in a crew to fumigate the house or room where that person had been living. The result of this effort was an almost immediate and a drastic reduction in the number of yellow fever cases in Panama.

It took a while longer, but Gorgas was eventually almost as successful in his efforts to reduce the number of malaria cases. He reduced these cases by not only attacking mosquito egg-laying spots, but also by clearing all the brush and trees from around human settlements. This helped because malaria mosquitoes, Gorgas learned, need shadowy places to stay during the day. The open areas around settlements, then, acted as buffers against malaria by preventing a new crop of mosquitoes from coming in from the jungle after the old crop had been killed.

In the long run, Gorgas did not completely win his war against mosquitoes. Though he temporarily stopped yellow fever and reduced malaria enough to allow the canal to be finished, Panama still had millions of mosquitoes when he left. Today, decades after the development of powerful insecticides, there is still malaria in Panama and, once in a while, a case of yellow fever.

The same is true in almost all the parts of the world that were ravaged by these diseases. There are fewer cases of malaria in most parts of the world and far fewer cases of yellow fever worldwide. But the diseases and the mosquitoes that spread them are very much alive—like a bed of hot coals that could burst into flames.

A MOSQUITO LARVA
SUSPENDED IN POND WATER.

Since Gorgas, the fate of these diseases has actually been up and down. With the development of powerful insecticides such as DDT, it was once thought that *Anopheles* and *Aedes aegypti* mosquitoes would be so successfully controlled that malaria and yellow fever would virtually disappear from the face of the earth. Gradually, however, both these kinds of mosquitoes began to develop an immunity to insecticides. At the same time, there were efforts by environmentalists to stop the use of insecticides, particularly DDT, because of the threat they were said to pose to different forms of wildlife.

The result, at least in some parts of the world, has been a recent explosion of malaria and some large outbreaks of yellow fever. Even in Panama, where Gorgas and his men fought so hard, malaria is making a strong comeback. Today, the battle between mosquitoes and humankind continues to rage.

GENERAL WILLIAM GORGAS,
THE MAN WHO PROVED THAT
YELLOW FEVER IS INDEED
TRANSMITTED BY THE
AEDES AEGYPTI MOSQUITO.

Chapter 8
Army Ants

This last great killer insect, the army ant, is one of the most frightening of all insects. And yet, it is actually one of the least dangerous insects mentioned so far.

The explanation for the awesomeness of these small, otherwise harmless-looking insects lies in the fact that they move about in huge numbers. Up to 20 million of them sometimes crawl around together, nibbling, pulling, tearing—*eating* everything alive in their path.

Here is the way a famous British scientist, Henry Walter Bates, described some army ants he saw in South America back when these insects were not well known:

> Wherever they pass, all the rest of the world is thrown into a state of alarm. They stream along the ground and climb the summit of all the lower trees searching every leaf to its apex. Where [food] is plentiful, they concentrate all their

forces on it, the dense [formation] of shining and quickly moving bodies, as it spreads over the surface, looking like a flood of dark red liquid. All soft bodied and inactive insects fall an easy prey to them, and they tear their victims in pieces for facility of carriage. Then, gathered together again in marching order, onward they move, the margin of the [formation] spread out at times like a cloud of skirmishers from the flanks of an army.

To get the full picture of what a swarm of army ants looks like, imagine a tide of them up to 33 yards (30 m) wide moving through the jungle at speeds up to 38 yards (35 m) an hour. A swarm this big makes a crackling and hissing sound in the jungle somewhat like rain coming through the trees.

The eerieness of a swarm of army ants is increased by the fact that, en masse, they have—just as their name suggests—a distinctly military appearance. In fact many species of army ants travel in a classic pincher formation that is shaped something like a *V*. This pincher formation allows an army—of people or ants —to encircle an enemy and fall upon it suddenly from all sides.

A feature of army ants that makes them so dangerous is their constant hunger for fresh, live food. Unlike ordinary ants, which usually scurry about looking for bits of dead food, grains of sugar, fresh leaves, and so forth, army ants kill what they eat. Their diet includes anything that comes in their path—grasshoppers, baby birds in a low-hanging nest, lizards, snakes, and rats. There have even been reports of army ants attacking penned livestock and, within minutes, tearing whole cows to pieces.

With these kinds of reports, it's not hard to believe the occasional story of a person falling prey to army ants. This horrid thought of a person being devoured by carnivorous ants is the inspiration behind a short story called "Leningen Versus the Ants."

Later made into a movie starring Charlton Heston, the story about Leningen deals with a Brazilian planter whose home and buildings become surrounded by a massive swarm of army ants. After fighting off the ants for hours, the farmer makes a run for a nearby dam to turn on a valve that will let water pour through and flood the area, and thereby drown all the ants.

By the time he arrives at the valve, however, he is covered with ants. As he runs back, fleeing both the ants and the rising water, his face becomes bloody with ant bites. He stumbles, falls, and almost gives up when he spots beside him on the ant-covered ground the ghastly remains of a deer that the ants have picked clean in only minutes. The sight so horrifies him that he staggers to his feet and manages to leap back across a water-filled ditch. Behind him, the water rises and destroys all the ants.

Though pure fiction, the story underscores the fear that these insects inspire in people who see them. The story also points up the reason army ants are included in a book about killer insects. In the right circumstances, they can and do kill people in a grotesque and horrible way.

The instrument army ants use to kill their prey are scissorlike mouthparts called mandibles that open and shut sideways. One of the most powerful insects in the world for its size, an army ant is capable of snipping a grasshopper's leg right off with one quick bite. One bite can also cut a tiny gash in a snake or a person. Obviously when a million or more army ants swarm over a living animal, they make very short work of it.

Fortunately, army ants are found mostly in Africa and South America in regions where few people live. Almost certainly, this is the major reason army ants aren't a bigger threat to human life than they are.

Chapter 9
More
Killer Insects

With close to one million kinds of insects flying about the world, you can be sure that quite a few more of them are killers than tsetse flies, mosquitoes, some bees and wasps, oriental rat fleas, and army ants. Exactly how many more are killers is not known since more are presently being discovered. Just recently, for example, scientists found a deadly insect in Israel that no one had ever studied before.

Called *Holotrichius innesi,* this near-relative of the bedbug has a bite deadlier than a cobra. Fortunately, it lives in only a few desert areas of the Middle East where people rarely go. The chances of this insect's ever becoming a major killer are therefore very small.

The same can be said about the following insects. All of them can and do kill people, though not nearly as many as the insects discussed earlier.

SCREWWORM FLY

This harmless-looking green fly, native to the southern United States and the Central and South American tropics, makes its deadly attack in one of the grisliest ways imaginable. It swoops down on a sleeping victim—always during the day—and quickly lays eggs near an open wound. Sometimes it will deposit its eggs near an infected ear or a runny nose.

These eggs (up to 300 can be laid in five minutes) quickly turn into tiny worms, or larvae, that crawl directly into the open wound or hole in the body. Once inside, they eat their way deeper and deeper into the body—through cartilage and finally into bone.

The danger is greatest when the screwworm fly has laid its eggs near a victim's ear or nose. Larvae that enter the body through the nose or ear often eat their way directly into the brain of the victim, causing delirium, fever, intense pain and, finally, a horrible death.

Fortunately screwworm infestations are rare today except in areas where there is poor sanitation and housing. More fortunate still, doctors can now treat screwworm infestations and kill the larvae long before they eat their way into the brain.

Even so, there are still some deaths every year caused by the screwworm. Invariably, they are truly horrible deaths.

BODY LOUSE

Seen under a magnifying glass, this small wingless insect looks a little like a monster. Protruding from its head when feeding is a nasty-looking mouth specially designed for drilling through skin

THE SCREWWORM FLY.

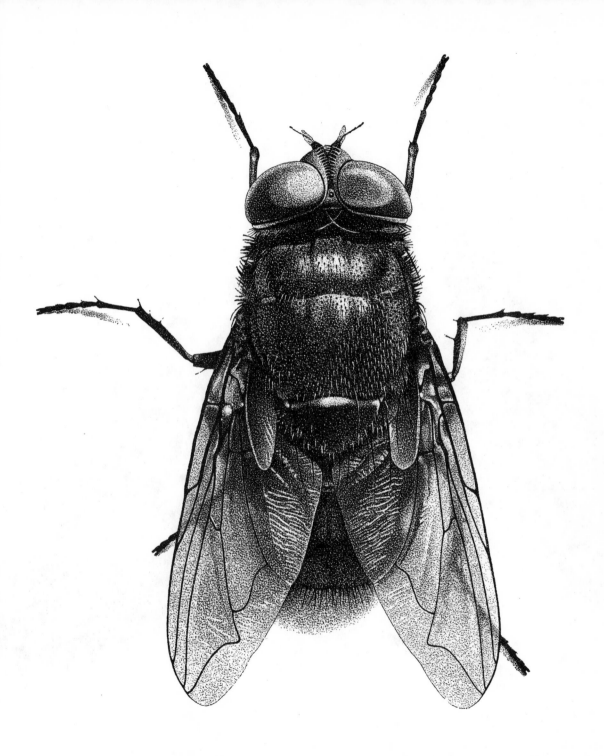

and sucking blood. The claws on its legs are specially designed for grasping human hair as it crawls about.

Body lice, known and despised the world over, are responsible for spreading a disease known variously as jail fever, war fever, spotted fever, or—more correctly—typhus. This disease is linked in name with prison and war because it tends to break out only when many people are forced to live together in dirty conditions. Over the years, it has often broken out, for example, in rundown prisons, in dirty army barracks, and in refugee camps.

Body lice spread typhus much the way other killer insects spread other deadly diseases—that is, they bite an infected victim, become infected themselves, and then bite another victim. It's important to note, however, that a louse cannot infect a person directly by biting as can, say, a mosquito. A louse infects a person only by way of its feces.

Typhus travels from one person to another, for example, when an infected louse defecates near the spot it bites. The bite of the louse hurts and irritates the victim so much that he or she scratches hard enough to break the skin and smear a tiny bit of louse feces into the broken area.

Though less horrible in some ways than the screwworm fly, the body louse is nonetheless an insect to be dreaded. In large numbers, even uninfected body lice can cause terrible suffering.

KISSING BUG

The popular name of this insect suggests that it is a nice, harmless creature. Actually, nothing could be farther from the truth.

MALE (LEFT) AND
FEMALE BODY LICE.

One of its other popular names—assassin bug—is closer to the mark.

The kissing bug is an avid bloodsucker that preys on people at night and gives them a sometimes fatal illness known as Chagas' disease. The name "kissing bug" comes from this insect's habit of biting people on the cheek, usually near the eye or mouth.

Kissing bugs are found in almost all the countries of Central and South America, as well as in parts of the United States. Luckily, they don't prey on people in all these countries. In fact, they are a problem only in underdeveloped parts of the Americas, where poor housing allows them to crawl freely between cracks in walls. It is from such cracks that kissing bugs usually launch their nightly attacks on people.

These cracks, however, serve another purpose too. They allow kissing bugs easy passage to the out-of-doors where they can become infected with the organism that causes Chagas' disease. The animals that carry this organism in the wild are rats, oppossums, and armadillos. In some circumstances, dogs, cats, and even guinea pigs can become a carrier of this organism.

An unusual thing about Chagas' disease is its tendency to be serious only when it strikes children. Most children who die from it are under two years of age. Adults generally suffer very little if they get Chagas' disease. Only about one percent of adults infected even show enough symptoms to go to a doctor.

Certainly, then, the kissing bug is one of the oddest of all killer insects. With a name that suggests *affection,* it actually preys on children at night and spreads *infection.*

THE KISSING BUG. ITS NAME COMES
FROM ITS HABIT OF BITING THE
TENDER PARTS OF THE HUMAN FACE.

For Further Reading

Blassingame, Wyatt. *The Little Killers: Fleas, Lice, and Mosquitoes.* New York: G. P. Putnam's Sons, 1975.

Callahan, Phyllis, S. *Insects and How They Function.* New York: Holiday House, 1971.

Graham, Ada, and Graham, Frank. *Bug Hunters.* New York: Delacorte Press, 1978.

Patent, Dorothy H. *How Insects Communicate.* New York: Holiday House, 1975.

Index

About the Author

Don Causey is Executive Editor of *Outdoor Life*, a magazine about hunting and fishing. An outdoorsman and traveler, he first became interested in deadly insects when he visited the Amazon jungle in South America.